Neuro Typical

A tale of four brothers
50 per cent autistic
(mathematically speaking)

By
S. Herbert

**Grosvenor House
Publishing Limited**

This book is published by
Grosvenor House Publishing Ltd
Link House
140 The Broadway, Tolworth, Surrey, KT6 7HT.
www.grosvenorhousepublishing.co.uk

A CIP record for this book
is available from the British Library

ISBN 978-1-83975-788-4

Graphic design: Nawal Arafat

For any child and family blessed with anomaly

About the author

The author, a veteran journalist, has made contributions to print journalism including the *New York Times Magazine*, *Vogue*, the *Saturday Telegraph Magazine*, *Evening Standard*, *Architectural Digest*, *House and Garden* and *Wallpaper** magazine, where she retains an editorial position.

A specialist in the fields of design, architecture and art, the author has frequently curated exhibitions in public museums and private galleries in London, Milan and New York, and most recently in the Middle East.

An award-winning furniture designer for the US hospitality marketplace, she has built a reputation as a pioneer in exposing as well as creating honest contemporary design. A seasoned author, her first book won a fiction award in the US despite not being fiction, and this and subsequent titles on her field subjects have been translated into numerous languages, including French, Italian, Spanish, Dutch, German and Russian. She has also presented television and radio on both sides of the Atlantic.

Mother of four sons, the author now lives in London, her birthplace, having straddled New York and Paris for a period of time. These latest writings provide a very different backdrop to her story.

"Every time I meet Suzanne and hear her stories, I wonder how she manages her wonderfully chaotic, fulfilling and atypical, world travelling, always-on-the-go existence full of sons, business, writing, friends, ex-husbands, a crucially important cat and other accumulated cast members of her life. I couldn't do it. I don't know anyone else who could. It's good to be able to find out just how it's done from the master."

Simon Lederman, BBC radio

Contents

Preface

Neuro Typical is a free-flowing autobiographical account – an ongoing story of what it is like for an already obtuse family to live around mental illness, relentlessly. Prompted by my 24-year-old son's comment, "Mum, you have no idea how privileged you are not to have mental illness", I have decided to write, in real time, our journey as a family today, while making references to the adventures that have brought us to our current situation, the voyage an ongoing plethora of peculiarity. You see, two of my other sons in the household are autistic.

Neuro Typical is written in a positive narrative style, as an intentional unstructured diary, which includes memories of the past, and explanations of past actions which counterbalance the "live" accounts. All events, past or present, are true, at least from memory, and the voices of all the participants in the book are written as heard with the intention of being honest and real. Where there are differing accounts of the same events, these stem from a difference of perspective due to the natures of the minds my children, the protagonists, have been "blessed" with.

The life experiences and perspectives of the participants, my children, reveal a complicated and unusual family set-up, the coping mechanisms, and the stances adopted, some organic, others knee-jerk reactions, that have helped to create a sense of normalcy to counterbalance a very confusing, to my boys at least, outside world.

Many experiences have been highly amusing and equally as many unfortunate and tragic, and all accounts come together through texts revealing a story that will shock as many readers as soothe others, from those who have no experience of mental illness, and those who deal with mental illness on a day-to-day basis. Many are affected.

The account is not a general nor lengthy explanation of mental illness itself, although the specifics of the mental illness we have encountered are explored in some depth.

My voice, the author, as storyteller, first and foremost gives a mother's heart-felt perspective – what it means to begin to acknowledge the differences in front of me, and then to have to bring up such a brood within a very urban, hard and fast environment, that covers everything from dealing with the health service and authorities on one hand to nurturing a family to create home comfort on the other, while at the same time trying to balance the necessity of having to work in a field that feels the polar opposite, and what can seem, publicly, like a life of glamour within an intense creative industry.

Through my family's personal anecdotes, and my sons' own personal traits and opinions, including those of my mentally ill son, our story, which has remained private until now, reveals itself. *Neuro Typical* delves into the minds of all four sons, including my two autistic sons, one an adult and one 14 years younger, who have, despite their own societal differences and unique problems, their very personal takes on living with a sibling with mental illness – severe OCD and reactive depression – alongside the experiences of a fourth teenage son, who is "normal".

There has been nothing "normal" about my children's experiences of the world thus far, and the writing style reflects the madness and syncopation of a highly unusual set-up, which nevertheless has been manageable, our way.

We, as a family, inhabit a world where expectations have had to shift constantly, where conforming became anathema.

As a writer focusing on the arts, as well as being a designer and exhibition curator "on the international stage" apparently, public speaker too, not to mention the TV and radio appearances (whoever the person over there is who actually does that stuff – is it really me, I wonder, as I crash to sleep each night?), the challenge to bring up my misfit family alone (not by choice or design, just circumstance) has been enormous. Another part of the story addresses finding a balance between work and home life, without entirely losing the plot myself, and being able to afford the shoe leather. "Smile, please" from the photographer in the second allowed on the "step and repeat" platform still offends my ears, when I have only just managed a sweep of lipstick and pull-on frock and thrown the children a half-decent supper.

Ned, as he is called (I use middle names, as agreed with "Ned"), my son who has been ill with severe mental illness for over 10 years since a pre-teen, is the most vocal of the boys, as he vehemently darts in and out of the narrative in inverted commas, partly, in reality, from the nature of his obsessive illness. His voice tells the inside story; what it is like to live within his own head, his experiences of hospitalisation and "sections", the medication, and then just being a boy with such a label and all that entails. Just being a boy.

Neuro Typical is written against the backdrop of the internet age, social media and all it offers, with both positive and negative outcomes, where even buying online has its consequences, and within a confusing enough world where parents and offspring are attempting to meet in an ever-developing technological era.

It is a simple modern tale nonetheless inspired by some of the literary greats written when mental illness and "deficiency" was less understood, from Faulkner's *The Sound and the Fury* to Steinbeck's *Of Mice and Men*.

There have been some great depictions in literature of autism in the last decades, though Mark Haddon's *The Curious Incident of the Dog in the Night-Time*, as well as *The Reason I Jump*, an endearing short tome revealing the inner mind of a Japanese autistic teen, Naoki Higashida, and very recently explorations into mental illness in contemporary literature, John Green's much awaited *Turtles All The Way Down*, where the protagonist clearly suffers a form of obsessive compulsive disorder, and *Eleanor Oliphant Is Completely Fine* (Gail Honeyman), a sensitive tale of a lonely woman's inner workings and her mother's mental illness, the latter two being fictional works. All incredibly worthy – chapeau to all.

In the "twenty twenties", when mental health is on everyone's agenda, from the housing crisis (how many mentally ill people are homeless?) to stigma, to the onslaught of pressures from social media to "pressure vanity" and the youth being driven to despair through peer pressure, how do we address the future of our loved ones? And the future of theirs?

Neuro Typical does not approach these issues directly but hopefully delivers some resonance, as it offers a genuine insight into both the internal and external machinations of dealing with mental illness in an extremely modern world.

Our story is set in London, and very London centric, gives a platform and grounding to an emotive tale that could be set anywhere. Souls are bared. Mine particularly.

This short tale will be controversial, for its content and because in my family world we are pretty un-PC about our terms, conditions and opinions – it goes with the territory. Nothing is sugar-coated. Everything is literal, thanks to the autistic boys. They have taught us a lot about the "here and now" and telling it straight. "Ned" (now an adult, not autistic) in particular wants to come clean. His hero is Stephen Fry (in part for his stellar intellect, but mostly for his open admission of mental health problems).

Above all, *Neuro Typical* is a crime of passion.

Neuro Typical
by
S. Herbert

Intro

We all have a public face and a private life. But when my 24-year-old son said to me earlier this year, "Mum, you have no idea how privileged you are not to have mental illness", we decided together as a family to use that privilege to go public and tell our story.

I have four sons, who have always lived with me, and who I have supported fully through my work in the creative industries, two born in Paris from my first (ex) husband, and two born in London from my second (ex) husband, and we have a beautiful black cat, Pepsi, who is very important to our family story with regards to one teenage son and his rehabilitation, whose childhood, in his own words, has been stolen. You see, my third son is "normal" in our personal chaotic world, and he needs some attention. He just doesn't know what "normal" is. Pepsi is his solace.

My eldest son, also in his mid-twenties, once said to me as I scrambled through their four Christian names before reaching the right one, a common deficit to all parents of multiple offspring, "Why don't you just give us numbers according to birth?" So, for the current purpose, I shall, along with the official labels:

Theo, number one, autistic
Ned, number two, severe mental illness since age 10
Eugene, number three, neuro typical
Beau, number four, autistic

I had my last baby naturally at 45 and people ask, what is it like to have a baby at 45? Well, that is just fine, but having a feisty 13-year-old autist at 58 is quite another, though I would not give up any of it for the world. I had an after-school nanny for my youngest,

Beau, a lovely Sri Lankan lady who came compulsorily with a wreck of a house I was renting from a friend with a closet in Monaco and a house in Bermuda. However, after a few years, she "found religion", which is understandable and was perfectly acceptable until the day my youngest ran off, as he often does, not realising he "belongs" to people, and instead of going to the information booth or the police in Victoria Station at rush hour, the nanny fell to her knees to pray for his return. I am afraid that was the end of that. My then six-year-old son managed to make sense of himself to an official who promptly put out an announcement.

At least having had practice with my eldest autistic son - and it is odd how we all adapt to speaking without inference and with logic within the autistic world - I knew not to tell my youngest son "not to speak to strangers" since everyone appears a stranger, but if lost to find someone wearing a hat, not a hood, and ask for help. This seemed the best option in London since hat wearers today appear mainly to be officials, at least 50 per cent of the time. The best odds I could find. The others, the cap wearers, must be rappers, I believe.

This is our story, told from the heart in all cases, and from strange and extraordinary minds in at least a couple. Although, as son number four asked recently, "How can something be extra AND ordinary? It just doesn't make sense."

Autism is not mental illness; it is a condition. Mental illness is quite another story. We'll begin with that. And end with "normal".

Chapter 1 Ned

My first incarceration came at 18.

I have been to plenty of hospitals over the years for CBT (cognitive behavioural therapy) treatment, but this was different. I went the morning after the Academy Awards, which I watch on TV with my mum. She loves the red carpet and I love the movies. The home care team, 24/7 at our house, sent in the shrink who suggested I should volunteer for the hospital and made it clear if I did not, I would be sectioned – talk about a catch-22. He fairly understood that sectioning would not be conducive to my recovery, since one of my greatest OCD fears is a closed door and corners, any corners, room corners, which I fear, and I need to pace and make movements as part of my "habiting". I am 6ft 5in, lanky, and I need to stretch and move. It looks like a dance, but it is my head, not my legs. I am not dangerous nor a criminal, maybe dangerous to myself with my thoughts, but it was advised because my two younger brothers were not supposed to bear witness to my "behaviour" anymore. They hadn't ever seen anything else, but I was an adult now. More the shame since that meant the adult unit, adult mental health.

I am in pain every day I live. Every day is agony. I cannot filter out information, so everything I see and hear has the same weight, and I create habits to stop the noise.

Unit 2 is where the loonies go when the docs don't know where to put them. It's like Vegas with better security. No clocks, no schedule, just a constant stream of punters, arriving mainly in ambulances and police cars around the clock. Day and night become one. The nurses in the mixed "ward" doling out the medication non-stop from a small office. It is a scene like something from the *Hitchhikers Guide to the Galaxy: The Restaurant at the End of the Universe*. It wasn't unenjoyable. There was ping pong. There were people.

I cannot close my door but don't want things touched either. The dribbling kleptomaniac still comes into my room and eats my food from outside, biscuits that Mum has brought in, and steals my clothes. That's serious CBT. I cannot shower, and I cannot clean my teeth: the habits take too long and other people need the shower. Mum visits, but the children are not allowed in, so I go to a small family room to eat McDonald's with my brothers. She cleans my teeth. That saves time.

Back on the ward, we play Cluedo. The old Indian lady who thinks she is impregnated by the devil – she has no or rotting teeth – clearly delusional, was finding it hard to grasp the central objective of the game but was determined to discover Miss Scarlet's motives. Another older lady, around 70, who reminded me of my grandmother, with her sigh and rasp of voice (I thought it was unique to my beloved grandmother), was seriously depressed like Eeyore the donkey (I realised watching other loonies that all of *Winnie the Pooh* is based on mental illness). She had no enthusiasm for the game but sighed in a winsome way through it

3

nonetheless. The catatonic young black guy, who appeared completely normal but couldn't speak, sat at the table on the instruction of the nurses and was clearly engaged in his own way, I guess, because he sat there. I couldn't roll the dice for fear of contamination, so the other young person, a suicidal and self-harming Irish girl with deep welts in her arms, who was really nice with long brunette hair, rolled for me. I hope she is OK. I fancied her a bit.

Movie night was fun. At the screaming behest of the toothless Indian lady, and to keep the ward quiet, the nurses would play some of Elvis Presley's best live performances – particularly the one in Hawaii. Hawaii seemed a long way from Wandsworth. What would Elvis have thought? He couldn't even take a plane to England because of his fears.

I was in Unit 2 for six weeks in order to give my brothers, and my mum, a break. There was no treatment, except the meds, but good crowd control, and it was safe. And it did get me into the programme for specific treatment later on. In all, I spent 10 months in the mental hospital that year. Sectioned a few times too for trying to abscond. My A levels in Philosophy, English Lit and Film Studies were on hold, although I had completed many of the papers and had fair grades – and I qualified for a scribe, so that helped. The school wouldn't keep me either. I needed to be kindly pushed through door thresholds by fellow students to enter a study room. It was affecting too many people, my fears and my habits. Space is a problem for me and thresholds and corners and intersections – where things meet. I have a mortal fear of intersections. They terrify me.

I was home for a difficult three months, but it could have been nine. Offered a place in the OCD Unit official at the loony bin whenever a place came up, to qualify, I had to go on a completely different medication system. It is a rule for qualification – you have to have tried two methods of medication for three months each to qualify. The second was a disaster; I looked as if I was tripping and the police picked me up once, thinking I was a dealer – the long hair also – I won't cut my hair in a bad state until I feel better. It is the same with clothes. I have to wear different clothes according to how I feel. It takes ages to dress. On, off, on, off, habits with my eyes rolling, head tilting and making sure I don't see a corner. It can take hours. Forget shoelaces.

I am on a waiting list – waiting for what exactly?

Mum had to go to the Middle East to work and before she left, she said jokingly to the hospital, "If there is a cancellation, we'll take it!" Mum has always had a sense of humour about our lot.

And there was one, next day, against all odds. First time. They called Mum in Dubai, and she flew home on the first plane out to gently break the news to me. I have severe OCD for Christ's sake, and I had to prepare for treatment the following day. This was not the plan.

God kill me.

Chapter 2 Shoe Shopping

Moving as a pack can be challenging, shopping for shoes almost an impossibility. When we move together, say to the Farmers' Market at 10 sharp on a Saturday morning, we are a motley crew. Little Beau has to dress for every occasion in a mini pin-stripe suit, button shirt, bow tie and black Velcro shoes (he will wear one pair of shoes until too small and they have to be replaced with the same. Clarks must never go bust). Quite a proper gentleman. He must have seen it on TV (Beau watches *Doctor Who* relentlessly). A suit is his uniform – and everything has to be uniform. We look like an Amish family shuffling to harvest with our recycled canvas bags, four boys walking in step, with the anomaly of tall Ned who cannot seem to negotiate a pavement without a jig or two, dancing backwards and forwards, retracing his steps. He doesn't avoid the cracks though – that is a common stereotype about OCD, almost a myth. It is a lot more complicated than that.

"How exactly did you make this bread, and how long did it sit for?" asks little Beau, without making eye contact, of our California-dude bread maker from Putney who always makes the journey to the Battersea market, he says, to say hi to my boys, as well as to sell bread. Very Blanche DuBois, we have always relied on the kindness of (some) strangers, and we always talk to strangers since (repeat after me) everyone appears to be a stranger to an autist. He does at least engage Beau for a few minutes, already behind the stall sorting and counting the coins for California-dude so I can focus on the next purchase and have time to actually taste the goats' cheese I think I would like to buy. California-dude is a kind man. He sees it all. We recognise them when they come along, and they become family too. A kind of molecular, as opposed to biological, family. Many strong, but distant, bonds. Beau introduces Mum as Suzie Sherbert, a name he made up, being unable to pronounce my real surname – his is different.

Mr "Normal", Eugene, a mid-teen, is mortified on every occasion – "That sounds like a hooker's name" – plugged in to his almost invisible earbud headphones and wearing the latest hoody he has found, negotiated and purchased on Depop along with rare Adidas Kanye-West-designed Yeezys won through some kind of expensive online lottery. Quite an entrepreneur buying and selling, he has a keen eye for internet fashion and a deal (at least I think so, since the packages keep arriving, sometimes only to be repackaged and sold on) – I hardly notice what he is up to. Pretending not to be with us, he nevertheless always watches my back in case something goes wrong, and it often does. Far too old for his years through necessity.

The autists, Theo and Beau, the largest and smallest of the motleys, think in slices of time. Everything is here and now, so crossing a road is a worry, as if a car cannot be seen or heard, it probably doesn't exist.

With autism, one of the main notable differences is in anticipation, the lack thereof, and empathy, the lack thereof. Inappropriate "behaviour" as a result. And clothing. Faces cannot be read, expressions have to be learned with special needs teachers (we have encountered scores of dear, caring people): "When someone looks like this - smiley emoji - they are happy. When they look like this - emoji with mouth turned down - they are sad" - "so what about …(pause).. when they look like this ?" - emoji with square grin - "not sure, what do you think Beau?" - pause - "I have been to the dentist?"

We walk everywhere, often misunderstood on public transport where commuter glares are just too much to bear, the autists on foot happily mapping out the path through urban trig points high up, the buildings, the architecture. I had a car, a Volvo XC90, large enough for the family, but sold it overnight on eBay last summer to the first available buyer. The responsibility of a car in central London, along with parking tickets (since everything takes longer with the motleys), was just a sandwich too far in my own personal picnic.

They say one in four people in the UK has a mental illness. Well, in my household, only one in four can tie their shoelaces.

Theo may go to bed balancing chemical equations for his amusement in his brain, but he cannot deal with shoelaces.

Through the right support, he did manage A levels in Maths, Chemistry and Biology. Physics he couldn't "get" in an advanced manner because of the "assumption" required. And he favours Velcro – adult size 11. Very difficult to find, and we shop hard for slip-ons. But he has a high instep, as do all my chaps.

Coupled with Ned's (also adult size 11) inability through "irrational fear" AKA OCD to delve into a basement of a shop, where men's departments flourish, or enter an elevator on any occasion, shopping for shoes is a tough call.

Chapter 3 Downsizing

Little Beau runs very fast, at least in straight lines, and not from anything nor to anywhere, although there has been the odd mission, just runs. If he is not running, he is jumping up and down, occasionally spinning, which seems to give him much comfort, and static when in front of a machine, which is a relief (communication with or through technology and visiting virtual reality seems easier than human reality for him). At this stage, I would like to formally thank the makers of *Minecraft* for their contribution to my family's wellbeing. I would also like to thank the makers of *Grand Theft Auto* for getting us out of a fix when lost in a rental car in a downbeat Los Angeles suburb. Theo, from memory, managed to navigate the streets having played the game online, and we found ourselves arriving at the Griffith

Observatory with great aplomb and to a huge round of applause from the motleys.

Education was designed by concrete linear thinkers, and I am afraid in this abstract household, I leave the reading, writing and arithmetic to the specialists. Our home education comes through boardgames and activity – they all play chess with focus – cycling, swimming, museum visits and early *Top Gear* repeats. Homework does not happen at home, for so many reasons, and I have always found it an anathema in any case. What are schools for?

Our own old decrepit rented "hot house" needed some navigation in itself and had four exit routes, including garden doors and a sash window, which Little Beau favoured for its efficiency. In summer, leaving exterior doors open was ideal for Ned, so he could come and go without the pain of threshold (we were there eight years). Yet, in time, we had to be mindful of Beau's newly acquired exploratory tendency. At the age of four, he decided to take a lonesome cycle ride around the park to find an appropriate picnic to join, which he did. It was a birthday party on rugs and, fortunately, one of the neighbours spotted him mid-popsicle and alerted the park police, who returned him home. My back was turned when making lunch, later than usual, and he was hungry.

On another occasion, he found a pound coin in the crease of the sofa, we now know, and trekked off to the local supermarket across a dual carriageway in his pyjamas and Wellington boots at seven in the morning to buy a Kinder Egg. I awoke that morning and he had disappeared. I ran to the neighbour, who ran around the park and called the police, and I darted to the supermarket, knowing it was familiar ground to him (instead of making lists of what he wants "at the shops", he draws intricate floor plans and has arrows pointing at the desired goods – Beau studies merchandising in case a product moves, which creates calamity), and there he was, already accompanied by Britain's finest, alerted by a fellow shopper as he was trying to pay. The "boys in blue" took him, and me, for a ride around the block a few times with the lights flashing, along with an accompanying lecture. He thanked them very much and said he would like to do it again sometime. The ride.

I realised that, unlike Theo, who was more static when younger, happy to sit and think and beam and smile at his own thoughts or sit and sort musical scores at the piano for hours on end, this one had to be watched.

Little Beau has a full Statement of Educational Needs, a minefield in itself to navigate and acquire but invaluable (Theo had one until 18) and had one-on-one support throughout the school day in his mainstream primary school, including lunchtimes. He had two carers per day, plus the lunchtime attendee. This meant peace of mind for the carers, one in the morning and another in the afternoon, who would find it exhausting if they had to attend to Beau for the full day. Now attending a "special" day school, he also has full disability allowance in his name, a contribution which butters our home care when I need a break and brings in a small rasher of bacon (not literally).

Beau is highly phototropic, and all of humankind is phototropic for survival, but with an autist's lack of understanding of time, this means he sleeps a lot in the winter but hardly at all in the summer, up with daylight and down at dusk. From the minute he wakes, he ricochets through the day, questioning everything around him. Despite the delay in speaking, he is now incredibly articulate and far too "precocious" for his years – in the old-fashioned sense – and each morning begins with a probing question and just doesn't stop. He has learned to "wait" thanks to a genius speech and language therapist who opted to use Lego as a device, recognising Beau's love of building, and invited others in the class to participate. One becomes the supplier of Lego pieces, one is the builder, and one is the engineer. The builder has to wait until the engineer asks the supplier for the required pieces. And together they sort, analyse, construct and fabricate. It works. We use the device at mealtimes, Mummy being the supplier.

Chapter 4 Alphabet Soup

A change in routine is a problem, and when Ned came out of the hospital after his longer sojourn, everything had to change.

After six months of official CBT (cognitive behavioural therapy) and the right medication in the right unit, Ned's OCD had shifted from "Severe" to "Mild to Moderate" and he had been told, gracefully, that he would always be ill, that his condition was chronic, and he just had to continue to use the methods learned and manage his life. This was a shock to Ned, whose adolescence had completely been engulfed by this creature within, but he was in a better place to understand. Being mentally ill so young affects maturity and his then 19-year-old comments to me, his mother, were more akin to those of a 15-year-old since his emotional development had been stunted. He was angry with me. His intellect, fortunately, stands him in good stead with friends and within his interests, although does nothing for the OCD itself, which, unlike many other mental illnesses, worsens with self-analysis since the "bad thoughts" just augment with rumination.

Still unable to function properly in a bathroom with a closed door and with his habit of tap turning, within a couple of months at home, the ceiling had collapsed in Theo's bedroom due to Ned's attempts to shower in a cubicle in a bathroom above, which meant banging against the glass door ritualistically and taking FOREVER (according to Eugene) in his ablution activities. If I wasn't home, taps could be left on for hours.

There was another bathroom, on a mezzanine, which became host to a ritualistic washing routine, but likewise, the ceiling of my office beneath came down one day through flooding. Eventually, Ned decided to shower in the garden using a hosepipe with only ice-cold water, come rain or shine, whenever the neighbours weren't watching, which was a huge relief to him. But it couldn't go on.

Fortunately, the friend with the closet in Monaco and a house in Bermuda decided the house needed to be sold or gutted in any case, and we were to move out.

In addition, the Community Mental Health team who visited weekly thought Ned needed to develop more personal skills and he interviewed for appropriate accommodation with various Trusts. Well enough to live alone, with a little help on the premises in case meds were forgotten, and for light support, but ill enough to qualify, again a dichotomy. The suggestion was to make him homeless to speed up the process, since we had to move anyway.

I broke the news to Theo, my gentle giant, who would also have to move on for practical purposes, and for his 21st birthday gave him a one-way ticket to the South of France to live with his father for a while, close to grandparents on that side and nearby a couple of aunts and cousins of a similar age. For any parent, letting one's children go is a wrench, but in this case, a careful and considered autist, to save the family, he had to go. And I had to make my child with mental illness homeless to boot. Two in one. In truth, I needed to downscale. I just hadn't been able to work as hard as usual nor travel so much, so cash was tight.

Then to find appropriate new accommodation there were criteria to adopt our plan. No more than three rooms total at least for a year or so – two bedrooms, one for me and the younger boys to share, ground floor with solid walls (noise), no basement (no underfloor neighbours). Small enough to be a tight unit but expansive enough for Beau's continual spinning and jumping, and a visible garden for Pepsi, Eugene's best friend, and Beau, with a gate that locks. In the locale for Beau's familiarity issues and on the park, with preference, for my view.

Sorted.

Chapter 5 Eugene

"I don't want to be Eugene. I want to be Dill. You don't have to protect me."

"And I like the story of why you gave it to me. How long's this book going to take? Are you writing about me now?"
(We are in the kitchen.)
"Not long, if you all stop butting in – just a few days."

Dill is named from Harper Lee's *To Kill a Mockingbird*. Eugene is his middle name, which he thinks is ridiculous.

"Are you sure? You are only a teen. You may regret it."

"I'm sure I am me... In any case, you always taught us no matter what happens to tell the truth, and we will sort everything out. I'm relying on you."

"This is interesting. It's like the Fourth Wall. Kevin Spacey is really good at it." (Ned)

"Was, you mean. Is he gay?" (Dill)

"Yes."

"What did he do?"

"Got off with a bunch of men, I guess."

"Isn't that what gay men do?"

"It's what lots of people do, and I don't think you can say gay anymore."

"What's going to happen to him?"

"Don't know... They wrote him out of that movie about the Getty with the cut-off ear, and the lady was paid less money than Marky Mark for the reshoot."

"Why was that?"

"Maybe she didn't want to make money out of Spacey's misfortune. Maybe she's a friend."

"How much did the other one get?"

"Millions."

"Why was that? Is he NOT a friend? Does he have to be careful too?"

"Maybe he had to cancel shooting another movie and wanted compensation. Things aren't always as they appear, Dill."

"Oh, I see…"

"Anyway, shut up. This bit is about me, right, Mum?"

"What are you going to talk about?" (Ned)

"Shut up."

"School? I went to the same school… Are you going to talk about me?"

"Not if I can help it. Read the title, dum chuck. It's about being normal."

Eugene, or rather Dill, does go to the secondary school Ned attended prior to Theo's arrival for his GCSEs, despite Theo's older age. It is a delightful and thoughtful small independent school nearby, founded by a man, formerly in finance, and his wife, who had dyslexic daughters and needed to think differently about their education rather than pigeonhole the girls into the system. They are good people. Every pupil is looked upon as an individual, and students thrive. The education is tailor-made according to skill and positivity. It is not a "special" school, and the attainments are fantastic, whether in arts, sciences or sport. Everyone has a place in the school, and we are blessed to have found it. It is a Christian school and having first seen the establishment, which frankly looks like a red-brick drive-through KFC (they are moving to new premises soon), I was entirely impressed and relieved to find somewhere where my quirky Ned would fit in. This was before the crash, his crash, and the eventual diagnoses (plural). This was perfect.

I listened to the head and the teaching staff and asked about the Christian ethos, which staff were happy to expand upon.

"Thank you so much for your time today. I think this is ideal for my son. Oh, and since Christianity was founded on the notion of forgiveness, forgive me for not being a believer, but do take my son. He will respect the ethos, and you are welcome to teach him about God and let him make up his own mind." And they did. As did Ned, who doesn't believe, although has mentioned Pascal's wager as a fallback – the philosopher in him speaking.

Theo was at a regular state school in Chelsea but not doing too well despite extra sessions and teaching assistants paid for by the council, so I went to see the council and requested the funds, which were quite substantial, instead of financing the school where, in a class of 30, Theo, with a surname ending in T too, was literally at the back of the class for alphabetic reasons, to be transferred into the private sector where there would be classes of 12 maximum. I was also aware as Theo was growing into a young man – this was year nine, before the two-year dash for GCSEs – he needed to be weaned off the kind of help he had been given since the age of five if he was ever to survive in the real world. He needed self-confidence.

At his state school (all the boys have attended local public primaries), it was thought Theo was good at

Cookery, Maths, Art Tech and Gardening. He had created an allotment at the school, which he tended at lunch and break times, in part because flowers and plants were his "friends" but, in reality, to avoid having to communicate with classmates in a social situation. Awkward.

Theo had one sport and a good one, archery, and he represented Kensington and Chelsea in the Youth Games four years in a row. Team sports only "neuro typical" Dill deals with and enjoys. Many autists who do not engage in competition just keep going until they get it right, and tenacity is never an issue. The task has to be completed. This quality, coupled with Theo's eagle-eye vision and his ability to mimic, meant he was a natural.

The council agreed after I put forth the reasons, said it would be good as a test case, although I sensed they were afraid the decision might open the floodgates. At the new school, it was that found Theo was excellent at Chemistry, Maths and Biology, when given enough time to focus and work at his own pace. Languages too, as well as Music. Theo has a keen ear for languages, mimics accents with perfection and takes them on as most of us take on rashes. Though his French, German, Spanish and Italian accents are impeccable, he nevertheless speaks "Disney" English. Not uncommon when small English-speaking autistic children's synapses are kicking in aged three. They frequently end up speaking with a vague American accent through watching age-appropriate films, many of which are made in the States.

"I thought this was about me, Mum?"

"It is."

Chapter 6 The Deal

"Mum?"

"Yes, Ned?"

Despite being newly housed in his "assisted living" accommodation in Tooting Bec, Ned visits daily if I am working from home (he doesn't have keys to my mini flat as part of the recovery "deal", because I am to become a mother again, not a carer) and inevitably suggests a pub lunch. He doesn't drink. "I have way too much chemistry going on as it is," he says. But he likes the "social", particularly with Mum, who pays and listens and, like Dill, watches his back. He also likes to go through the film scripts he has been writing with his new "scribe", a lovely Polish girl named Pola, only 19, who out of kindness and having seen him struggle to even walk along a pavement in a single direction, offered to help him out – typing would take forever with his "habits".

For all public exams, Ned qualified for an official scribe, which, as a method of working, to pass at A level is quite something of a skill to perfect. Never completing any homework through inability to put pen to paper, nor classwork for that matter, Ned throughout school and college would take a photo with his iPod of the white board, for his reference, listen with intent to all classes, rocking and rolling around as he does, contributing wildly and animatedly, and then manage to vocally spout a 3,000-word essay with quotes in the right places in a Philosophy exam, with references. All in exam conditions, enclosed in a room with a silent typist. Sometimes he had clever ploys. For his compulsory Religious Studies GCSE, he simply read the Gospel according to John, the shortest – or was it an audio book? – and memorised 25 good but generic quotes by the likes of Mother Teresa, Gandhi and Martin Luther King, which could be dropped into any essay and made relevant. Needs must. It was hard work. Both Theo and Beau possess eidetic memory, but Ned just has to remember his way, and without mnemonic, since that is yet another layer of mind flack. He took and passed four GCSEs by the age of 14, including Personal Finance "randomly", as the kids say.

"Mum!"

"Yes, Ned."

"Is it diegetic?"

"What do you mean?"

"Diegetic, you know. It can refer to music too."

"How?"

"You know, like Mel Brooks's *Blazing Saddles*, where an actual orchestra appears playing the music."

"Like in *High Fidelity*, where John Cusack is playing vinyl within the film, which becomes the soundtrack?"

"Not exactly. It's from the Greek. If you look at the third book of Plato's *Republic*, you'll see what I mean.

Lyric, epic, comedy and tragedy all relate events but by different means. You know, diegesis or mimesis…"

"Steak and chips, please, medium rare, and a pint of coke."

"I'll have the baked Camembert and a large glass of house white."

"Should you be having that, Mum?"

"Yes, I think I should. Have you taken your meds?"

"Oh, bugger."

Chapter 7 Cats and dogs

"A biologist, a statistician and a mathematician go into a pub and see an empty building opposite."

"Is this a joke, Theo?" asks Dill, nonplussed. Theo continues, oblivious to the puzzled look.

"They see two people go into the building and three people come out."

"Right."

"The biologist says, 'Oh look, they've reproduced!'"

"Ah ha…"

"The statistician says, 'Two and a half have gone in and two and a half have left.'" (Theo looking intent, delivering clumsily in broad Disney.)

"Uh?"

"And do you want the punchline?"

"Go on, thrill me."

"And the mathematician says, 'If one person goes into the building now, there will be nobody in the building.'"

"I get it, I get it!" shrieks Beau, jumping up and down with a hand-painted and still glue-sticky decoupaged cardboard box on his head with pinking shear cutouts for eyes.

"Zero, plus two, take away three, is minus one, plus one, makes zero."

Theo and Beau are dead chuffed. The sticky box comes off, and they coyly tilt their heads, no eye contact. Their version of a high five.

I like Theo's jokes, particularly the Latin ones, and we have to laugh again and again when he walks into a pub, holds up two fingers and says, "I'd like five beers, please." Always a winner.

Another maths joke follows. I'll spare you the full version, that begins, "Two mathematicians walk into a pub" and ends "and the barmaid says, 'Plus a constant.'" A little advanced for Beau's primary school maths, or any of ours for that matter, a diversion in hand.

"Theo, pop to the shop, darling, and buy four pints of milk, please."

"OK, Mum."

Theo is home for a couple of weeks from the South of France, missing the throng, feeling a bit sorry for himself, and having found a ticket on EasyJet for £9.99 precisely. Except it was from Toulouse, not Perpignan, where he now lives. Close enough. But there was, at least, a bus to Toulouse and a musician aunt who resides there – she plays the jazz scene – to ensure he made the plane. A bus from Stansted secured his delivery to Victoria Station, from where he lumbered with his backpack, thankfully the chimneys at Battersea Power Station newly restored in prime position for navigational purposes, and the entire exhausting journey costing less than two West End cinema tickets (popcorn excluded).

In Perpignan, historically a piratical port if ever there was, but a beautiful medieval town, Theo had just had his wallet stolen, which is why he was feeling a bit down. It is a small old town, the crux of it (it has its sprawl) quite chi-chi, with its fashion and luxury brands presenting in tiny quaint boutiques. Theo is known there now, volunteering at the local Brazilian dance centre and restaurant, independently taking tourists to the local attractions, churches and palaces whenever they seem lost, waiting on street corners for anyone pondering a map, using his multi languages. He is larger than life in the community and a mine of information, soaking up the history and expounding to all and sundry just because he can. Nothing official and no pay, just occupation. And he is very distinctive, certainly not an average-sized Frenchman. When in France, he is quite a giant with his curly but managed fairish hair and his beard, white ruffled shirts and the odd long frock coat, out of choice. What was it Jean Cocteau said about French men? They are born boys and grow old very quickly, and American men are born middle-aged and stay that way for life. I paraphrase, but Theo does look out of his time, and certainly his age group, in his own private pantomime of life.

"Was it a pickpocket?"

"No, he didn't pick anything."

It is a tourist town, after all, in French Catalonia, with mountains to one side and the beach to the other, and as happens with ports and borders, numerous peoples traverse through, often shafted by indigenous and transient crooks.

"So, what happened?"

Apparently, a homeless person Theo regularly gave coins to – he feels obliged – asked for money, and Theo decided to engage in polite conversation, said he had no cash, and took out and showed the contents of his wallet to prove the point, apologetically, which was indeed empty of cash. Opportunistically, the homeless person took the wallet, which carried English and

French debit cards, including the dreaded Contactless where money can be drawn swiftly in multiple units of £30-plus, and ran off with it. This action hurt Theo because he thought the homeless man was his friend, because there had been an exchange of sorts over time. It happened just outside of the apartment where he lives with his father, dead in the centre of the Old Town – more insult to injury. It should have been a safe place.

"Well done, Mum," says Dill, with struggling youthful irony, in his deep, newly broken voice, emptying a shopping bag Theo has just handed over to him containing four single-pint cartons of milk.

"Oh."

Dill and I smile. With Theo being away a few months this time, have I slipped, forgotten quite how literal I have to be with him? I should have asked for a "one four-pint carton of milk". With Beau, everything is so frenetic there is not even time to dwell on such matters, and the "speak" usually comes naturally, as naturally as possible, because of the Pavlovian conditioning, his to me. Communication with Beau is a marathon every minute of the day and you have to be on your toes. But having had the more placid, almost stoic Theo, 14 years before Beau was born, I shouldn't make these mistakes with him. I used to be more thoughtful. His solidity and kindness within the family unit is exemplary, and because Theo is so absolutely accommodating, he easily slips into the fabric. Must do better, me. Stop and think. Yes, I have had small children for a couple of decades, and I still have a young child as well as vulnerable young adult children. I should know better, take more care.

Excursions for teenagers are always a worry for parents and in Theo's teenage years, the wish, the kiss and a promise were all I could do when he decided to venture out on his own – as well as a deep breath. Theo has taken himself off in many directions, unbeknown to me at the time, and some of the developments have been life-changing for him and for us, his family, in understanding who he has become.

As a young teen, he once asked if I would attend church with him one Sunday at 9.45am precisely.

Theo's primary school was difficult to find – I left France when he was four with no prep this end – and the obvious, most convenient school choice would, at the time, not accept a child who seemed a little different. They were quite discriminatory. Theo did not have a formal diagnosis at this point, which comes best through the state school system in any case, so a foot in the door was needed. A progressive new headteacher changed all that a few years on, hence Beau's accommodation there – the first autist this particular Westminster mainstream school kept. Another primary school did take Theo eventually (it was the late nineties), a school with a decent and established Special Needs department, again in deepest Westminster, historically providing provision for the disadvantaged of London in the name of Baroness Burdett-Coutts, a 19th-century philanthropist whom Edward VII called "after my mother, the most remarkable woman in the Kingdom".

Theo, at primary school, made a friend in class who was the son of the vicar of the church attached to the school. They had music in common, and Theo began trying to find patterns in his friend, Michael's, movements, and attended church on Sundays to be alongside him. They played together, consistently and separately when together. The mum and dad, both vicars (how terribly modern), engaged Theo at every opportunity and invited him often to their home, the vicarage on Vincent Square.

In time, Theo became quite a part of the church community, attending Sunday School, becoming an "Older Hallelujah", joining the choir – eventually a baritone – assisting Tony the Verger in the maintenance of the church and setting up the hymn boards. Theo also helped at the door for parish lunches and usefully set up a numbered coat check system. Years later, I found he also, on the way to church, would collect an elderly lady in a wheelchair to help with her speed. None of which was ever mentioned. He would just leave the house every Sunday morning and go about his business.

So one Sunday morning, we attended church at his request to find, with utter surprise, that he was being confirmed that day, having had the requisite sessions for the confirmation. The whole affair was presided over by the then Bishop of London, Richard Chartres, who said to me following the ceremony – in just less than Brian Blessed tones – that he wished many of his flock, indeed his "work force", had half the in-depth understanding of the Bible as my son.

The coat check continued for a few years and Theo was offered a position as Assistant Verger when he left college, which meant a safe environment, and a job he juggled with night club door work and cocktail bar work elsewhere.

Another surprise excursion came when Theo was 17. I arrived home to a friend, former SAS G squadron, breaking a toothbrush in half in my kitchen – for less weight – and packing a rucksack. "Are you leaving?" I asked my houseguest. "No, Theo is." Fortunately, not for the SAS, the Foreign Legion, nor any advanced military activity.

A fellow sixth form student and friend, one of a cohort of four, had lost his life jumping from his parents' Notting Hill house. The teenager had laid out his passport, house keys, anything important, in a row on his bed, and jumped. No one had seen it coming, such is the fragility of young minds. James' parents then set up a fund for fellow students to apply for in the name of their son in his memory, and Theo had written applications and been awarded the fund for a trip, which he had described in detail in his application. He was going to Mont Blanc, climbing gear and all. He was to write about the experience for the college magazine.

I had to let him go, with his second-hand army issue kit ready, packed by an expert, but absolutely no experience in mountain terrain. He had been online with some Japanese men and women who also planned to walk and climb, and they had found a guide. He was to join their party and it was going to be gruelling, 20 kilometres daily with steep climbs and descents – not the easy route. It was a challenge for even the experienced, but I knew Theo's tenacity would keep him at it, as long as the boots fitted.

I took Theo to Gatwick Airport on the express train.

"It's raining cats and dogs."

"Aw, you can't fool me this time, Mum."

When Theo had first heard the expression, he looked out of the window to seek the cats and dogs falling, then researched the term and found some logic. It comes from the Greek "Cata Doxa", meaning contrary to experience or belief. Not just some odd, limey slang.

"In France, they say it's raining ropes."

He had organised a ticket to Chamonix, and a hostel. He would be back in a few weeks, and I made sure there was money in his back account and that the phone was on the European system.

Another deep breath.

"Do you know exactly where you are going, Theo?"

We were at Departures.

"Yes, Gate 22."

I had meant the hostel.

Theo was back in a few weeks, a week later than expected – his mother having kittens – having learned to paraglide as well.

Chapter 8 Kensington High Street (one Monday morning)

"Are you going to talk about your stroke, Mum?"

"Wasn't planning to, Ned, that's history."

"You should."

"Why?"

"Sharon Stone."

"I'd love those legs."

"She had a stroke and lost her side for a bit longer than you, and said she was damaged goods in Hollywood, and no one would touch her."

"Well, that's a shame. She is an icon for my generation and a pin-up for the entire second sexual revolution. You know, Ned, in Japan, when a fine porcelain artefact breaks, it is not disposed of but stuck back together with golden glue. The imperfections are augmented, and the piece has a new life, in a more fragrant manner, and lives longer than the rest because it is respected."

"Maybe there should be the Golden Glue Awards for all those actors."

"I was thinking about fragile actresses."

"You can be so uncool, Mum."

"Jane Fonda had a heart attack around 40, having just put out a whole bunch of workout videos looking great, now that was a shock, and she looks amazing now."

"That is a lookist comment."

"Lookist? When I saw the first *Shrek* at a premiere screening, I went with a fellow journalist, he was from *The Times*, who whispered at the end, 'Clearly the message of the story is that ugly people should stick together' – now that's 'lookist'. It was funny though."

"Yes, it is."

"Christine Keeler died recently."

"Who's that?"

"Another heroine of my time, quite a poster girl for those of us wanting to explore sexual freedoms – it's all so different now. My generation enjoyed a wolf whistle and a flirt and a few late nights with a groping good-looking male. Keeler was in many ways an inspiring role model for a continuing sexual revolution. She brought down the government."

"Intentionally?"

"No. The obits were billing her as a young woman groomed for sex with various MPs and one journalist, even said that, unlike Jane Asher, she came from the wrong side of the tracks and didn't know what she was doing, as if impecuniousness has any play in matters of the heart or ambition. I think she had a bad rap and history will reveal the truth eventually."

"Did she do it?"

"Do what?"

"Bring down the government?"

"No, it brought itself down. And there is this photo that appeared in all the press that week when she was meant to be a model, shot on an Arne Jacobsen chair – I'll show it to you. Well, I'll tell you something for nothing. That chair is a fake, it's not Arne, and the German photographer who took the shot said it was a publicity stunt for an upcoming movie about Keeler that didn't see the light of day, and something she wanted who knows. It's all in the V&A archives. Journalists today can be so sloppy. Now you want conspiracy theory…"

"Actually, I don't."

Chapter 9 Down the Tube

One January, half a dozen years back, the first school run of the year, I gave Beau, in his pristine school uniform (they still wear shorts in the middle of winter) hand to hand, to his carer at school, wished a resounding Happy New Year and walked to the tube. The train was just about to leave the platform, thankfully, and I jumped on in haste.

Emerging at Kensington High Street, walking up the steps towards the barrier, I felt out of body. I had not had breakfast and thought I was hungry – perhaps low blood sugar coupled with the daily early morning run of 5 to 10K.

Pret a Manger revealed itself, and as I tried to hold and pay for a chicken salad, my left arm fell, my heartbeat racing. I could hardly breathe, and I stumbled out of the tube station looking like a drunk before collapsing, consciously slipping down a glass shop vitrine as my left side went completely. I knew I was falling and wanted to protect whatever I could. I couldn't see either.

The vitrine belonged to Boots Pharmacy, how fortuitous, and the heroic pharmacist rushed out and knew exactly what to do. Moments later, the ambulance arrived, and I was "blue lighted" to the Stroke Unit at Charing Cross Hospital.

Ned calls it a "stroke of luck" because it didn't kill me (we know what is wrong – hereditary), and I have recovered. Meds forever, but thank goodness for the NHS.

The planets were clearly in alignment. A *Sliding Doors* moment if ever there was one. If the train had left, I would have taken the next one 10 minutes later and would probably still be going around the Circle Line, prepared for the new work season, dressed in Stephane Kélian platform boots and a snazzy vintage Gianfranco Ferré coat.

My destination had been the Design Museum.

"If you'd have made it there, Mum, you could have always claimed Stendhal syndrome – more up your alley."

"Thanks, Ned, for your vote of confidence."

Chapter 10 In or out

With physical ill health, there can be many varied misfortunes; a broken ankle, an annoying cough, the flu, short term problems, then the chronic, diabetes, arthritis, some genetic, and sadly the horrific cancers, tumours, embolisms, some ailments hereditary, others from birth, some developing as we go along, those taking us by utter surprise, others just passing us by, many curable, others not.

Mental ill health is the same, many ailments affecting us briefly, some significantly, others lifelong. So why the binary? Mentally ill or not mentally ill? In or out? It is simply illness and should be thought of as such, with, as happens at least in the First World if help is sought, carefully administered medication helping to take the edge off certain conditions, therapies, and medical care when necessary, hospitalisation when crucial, and none of it hidden (let's not even dwell on the impact to insurance companies). As well as mental health support for people, adults and children, caring for those who are ill, sometimes "critically" so. A word I use with regards to Ned, despite the "chronic" prognosis, because, in reality, I don't know how long he is going to be able to live within his mind, and neither does he.

It is a very broad arena, mental illness, and it is possible for us all to have a bout of depression. Help should always be sought because any depression can be debilitating for the sufferer and those near and dear. It certainly affects the workplace, causing a domino effect at times. None of it is embarrassing, but the stigma continues.

I am no doctor and will not attempt to make sense of the varieties of mental illness, but I am "privileged" to be able to read around the subject.

In 2015, The *British Journal of Psychiatry* reported a study that ambitiously tried to see whether differences could be found between disorders classically defined as being psychiatric versus neurological, based on brain anatomy. There are two main fields of medicine of the brain, one dealing with neurological problems, epilepsy, Parkinson's disease, multiple sclerosis and types of dementia including Alzheimer's – awful but not socially "embarrassing" – and then the psychiatric, the ones we don't talk about enough, which include depression, schizophrenia, PTSD, ADHD, OCD and autism.

So, in the quoted study, both types of disorders were found to be associated with measurable differences in brain anatomy. Fascinating for our family, the hippocampus, a structure invoked in emotion processing and memory processing, was often found to differ in size, compared to controls, in people with both neurological and psychiatric disorders.

Some of the differences discovered in the study showed psychiatric disorders implicating areas of the frontal lobe more than the neurological disorders. Other discoveries, however, were more surprising, such as psychiatric disorders being more associated with brain networks involved in processing visual information.

Overall, it was difficult for the authors to come up with a coherent "theme" to summarise the nature of psychiatric versus neurological disorders with regards to brain anatomy, other than to say that some differences were found.

It was stated, after what seemed to be an arduous and thorough study using MRI scanners, "We found that both types of disorders were associated with widespread alterations in cortical and subcortical areas."

And to conclude, there was a suggestion that perhaps the separate fields of neurology and psychiatry should be collapsed, as both specialties lay claim to the same organ. Well, let us not muddy that water.

American child psychiatrist David Rettew MD, from the University of Vermont, said about the same study "There may be other more legitimate reasons to keep the specialties distinct at least for now, and the brain is certainly complex enough to have lots of people looking out to keep it as healthy as possible."

I agree with the venerable doctor. The more heads on the subject, the better in a science that has a way to grow, neurological or psychiatric, unlocking the causes for mental ill health, and the treatment thereof. But I was pleased to find the accepted neurological disorders even mentioned in the same breath as the psychiatric. This a step forward to sorting out that "organ" – the "them" and the "us" linked by cortical and subcortical areas.

In a dream world, there would be an entire NHS specifically for mental health, the NMHS perhaps, which we all subscribe to and visit regularly for a check-up, an MOT, to break the stigma and to prevent a worsening situation. Like the six-monthly visits to the dentist, it should be routine.

Ned, with his severe OCD and subsequent reactive depression, takes medication and lots of it. As a young teen, he was prescribed 20mg of Sertraline per day, an SSRI inhibitor, gradually increased (he was undergoing CBT regularly too and under constant watch) to 50mg, then 80mg (the norm is under 50mg), increasing to 100mg in a couple of years. The odd antipsychotic drug was carefully thrown in for good measure when he had very difficult bouts, and frankly, finding the balance made Nurse Ratched's administrations look like those of a kindergarten teacher.

One imagines but hopes never to see an ageing parent fiddle in a pre-packed cellophane-covered dosette box for pills, in order not to confuse a daily dosage of medicine – alarming and an issue of dignity for all concerned. But, likewise, to see a teenage son with an armoury of chemicals just to keep him safe is simply sad. We had to accept, my son Ned and I, this was the way it was going to be.

Ned's morning cocktail now consists of 300mg of Sertraline, which is massive, and 250mg of Pregabalin, another mega dump, with daily breakfast Aripiprazole as the antipsychotic, and the night dosage means a further 250mg of Pregabalin. None of these knock him out – they just keep him ticking, functioning to a point. To knock him out, Chlorpromazine is on hand for emergencies, which as an adult, he now self-administers when he finds no other option and just needs to stop being in his head.

Final chapter OMG

"Hurry up, Ned, I'm freezing."

"FUCK, FUCK, FUCK."

"Muuum, Ned's caught Tourette's."

"No, I haven't, Dill, and you can't catch Tourette's."

"Seems you have."

"It's not Tourette's. I've stubbed my toe."

"Sure it wasn't your head on the way in? It took you long enough."

Ned has been circumnavigating the common hallway for some minutes now, in an attempt to enter my apartment, having buzzed the outer doorbell incessantly. Having made that initial threshold, he is at least now inside the building, so the outer doors can be closed behind him to keep in the communal warmth. Thank goodness I live on the ground floor, or time would take on quite another dimension.

He is negotiating the apartment entrance now proper, going in and out again and again in a crab-like sideways walk with his back to my bedroom door, having spotted a further crisis looming. I foolishly had left a light on – a lovely ornate hand-painted pinkish French lamp from my late mother's hoard, dating back to her antique dealing days – in the far corner of my otherwise modernist bedroom. My bedroom is visible from our internal entrance hall, and I usually close my bedroom door for Ned's swift passage past – nothing peculiar, not Oedipal. It is just a matter of a tight room corner he believes he will be sucked into unless he evades its vision. However, Ned arrived sooner than expected for an interview with police, and I didn't think quickly enough, and his nervousness and anxiety about the impeding meet, coupled with the ultra-illumination and a highlighted bedroom corner, is almost too much for him to bear. The film *1408* with John Cusack put Ned back months and became a trigger, something to do with the lighting in the hotel room. It's complicated.

The police arrive, or rather one policeman – his partner remains in a car outside.

"That's unusual," says Ned.

"It is unusual," says the policeman, emotionless as he removes his hat.

"Come on in."

Beau takes the hat as a cue to address the policeman.

"I am not lost. Has someone died?"

"No, Beau, not yet."

"Dill, stop it or I'll have them cart YOU off to the Yard."

"OK, Mum."

"Dill, will you take Beau and a box of Lego into the other bedroom, please. I don't care which theme, just be constructive, and see if you can occupy him for 20 minutes. I need to talk with Ned. You be the supplier and find an imaginary friend for the third party."

"OK, Mum, is it serious?"

"I don't know yet."

"Do you want me to stay, Ned?"

"Yes, please, Mum."

I had no idea what had led to the police engagement but assumed it was not terribly urgent since we were told of the visit hours ago and there were no blue flashing lights. Blue lights are good for us, unlike Marnie's red. Hitchcock's *Marnie* has significance in our home. She could not bear to be touched, and a flash of red gladioli or a splash of red ink on her sleeve sent her into a paroxysm of terror. We like the film. Our blue is the antidote to her red, usually signifying safety.

Ned had telephoned the police to report a crime the night before in the wilds of Tooting Bec, on foot, confused and cashless, and when the police said they would pay a visit earlier that day on the phone – Ned and I were having a lunch when the call came in – we decided it might be better to stay local to my home, which Ned was relieved by, not wishing to contaminate his new home with the memory of the emotional injuries of the night before.

The policeman began:

"This is a serious crime, and I have looked into your statement from late last night and see you are what is termed a vulnerable adult, and I have turned off my camera to talk to you."

"It was terrible. I was shafted," begins Ned.

"I am not going to arrest you."

"Arrest me? For what?" He blanched.

"Soliciting – it is an offence, and the law is changing faster than even we can keep up with. It's all the procurement issues with young girl immigrants and grooming and predators and organised crime."

"Ned, what happened for goodness' sake?"

"Mum, it's embarrassing."

"I should coco, but maybe we need to sort this out."

Ned's emotional development being thwarted by his illness has meant sexual development, not physical, but emotional sexual development, has not really had much play in his life and at 24, he remains a little cautious around girls, women, the opposite sex, any sex.

Facebook and social media, Snapchat, even Tinder, available to all, suggest there is plenty of action "out there" should a young man wish to meet a lovely lady, and many young men, and women, to meet a man (or whomever in this gender non-binary epoch), succumb, often successfully to meet their partner online. It has been going on for centuries, meeting through a third party, and for at least two decades online. I have a Russian girlfriend in Belgravia who when traded in (she received derisory fiscal compensation) by her oligarch husband for a younger model, went onto a very curious website costing precisely £10,000 to find a new husband, which guaranteed excellent service and had a great track record. Each morning after the school run,

I pass her new five-storey Belgravia house where she is happily ensconced with her new, slightly older English chubby hubby, very old school and secretive, his and her children away at boarding school, happily. Different strokes for different folks, but my Russian friend's resourcefulness and gamble was nothing but impressive. The Moonies have been doing it forever, marriage partnerships between strangers, and claim a divorce rate of just 5 per cent against the average 50 per cent within other "sectors". I know many men who use Tinder, and Grindr for that matter, successfully and at great speed (we all measure success differently), thankfully their smartphone navigational devices intact to complete the journey. I often think some of these men will pass their sell-by dates and wear out well before their smartphones, despite a built-in short shelf life (the smartphones).

Ned is a dab hand at making short sentences work for him, with it being too stressful to write anything longhand, and has learned to express himself pretty well through social media in the right places at the right time, with the right mindset. He managed to blog from the hospital at one point, with amusing content – even chatting up the odd "young woman".

"Where r u?"

"In my bedroom, look" the "catfish" (I am learning the jargon) posting a fake image of herself in half a negligée.

"And u r?"

"On the ward."

"R u doc?"

"No, patient."

Once, when I was in the UAE about to attend a Majlis in the presence of Her Highness, a Sheikha, and her entourage to discuss the UAE/UK Year of Cultural Collaboration and how we can learn from both cultures to support contemporary design (75 per cent of the Middle East is under the age of 35 and design culture is high on the agenda in encouraging the youth to go into the arts – after all, the oil and gas days are over – my brain is kicking in), I had a phone call from the hospital.

There were a few minutes remaining before the Majlis, a round-table-type discussion, was to begin, while protocol was sorted and before we took our positions, and the camera started to roll. I had my initial words prepared and was ready to ad lib according to the way the Majlis progressed. In my head, I rehearsed: "Your Highness, all design is communication, as language is communication. In Arabic, there is no word for 'space', as in spatial awareness, nor 'architecture' per se, just 'building', and no word for 'deadline'..."

I was primed and ready to go. But I answered the call:

"This is the hospital. Do you have knowledge of your son's whereabouts? He has absconded."

I could only accept certain important long-distance "gigs" when Ned was in care, which could be unpredictable to say the least. I felt awful and helpless and had to turn my phone off, and hours later would then attempt to find my son. At least my head behaved at the "gig". I was lucid enough, but my memory of it is in slo-mo.

Seemingly, Ned had managed to record a particularly noisy night in Unit 2 on his phone. It was a later incarceration than the initial episodes. The patients were rowdier than experienced before and Ned wanted to sleep. He then posted the wailings on Facebook to his entire group, asking anyone in the vicinity to break him out. One former schoolfriend, George, answered the clarion call, offered to help by meeting Ned with clothes and a rucksack, giving him an Oyster card and offering him a room for the night.

The psychiatrist had changed from the pair who signed the section papers, that time, and really thought Ned needed a break, so allowed him to walk in the grounds with a nurse. In Ned's cunning plan, he had left his iPhone with the other nurse on a charger so they would not think he would go far (phone chargers have to be kept in the nurses' station since they constitute ropes, which, along with plastic bags, are forbidden on the ward).

George, the old school friend, also aged 20 at the time, had enough nous to lend his phone to Ned, and the escapee called me later that day. I had to take a plane to deal with the fallout, but no real crime had been committed. Just a frightened young man with a Facebook audience. I took him home. The doctors let him off.

The night in question, back to Tooting Bec, Ned had been in a lengthy, yet text shorthand, expressive exchange using emoticons and monosyllables with a lady online, which apparently became rather fruity. Not Tinder, just a girl who popped up innocently through an online group meet.

They had talked about intimacy – not in the group chat, clearly – and Ned had made a suggestion that appealed greatly to the young lady, who seemed genuine at the time.

He had invited her to his new "flat", aware the care team were off at weekends – although he can have guests as long as they sign in, nothing untoward there – and she arrived, looking just like her picture. What a relief. Ned had tidied his quarters and made the bed, just in case. We have all done it as teenagers when our parents are off to a dinner party or "down the pub".

"You have to pay the taxi outside," she said.

"Oh, how much is it? I may not have enough cash."

"Forty pounds."

"Didn't know you lived so far away."

"Come, the driver will drive to a cash machine."

"OK," said Ned as he struggled to put on his shoes but remained composed to appear as normal as possible.

This is where he realised his mistake. As he entered the "taxi", the driver was on the phone and Ned, from the back of the car, saw the screensaver when the driver left the call, a photo of the young lady. They were clearly a couple.

In the back of the car, an alarmed Ned played the game. He went to the cashpoint, accompanied by the girl and her "driver", who insisted he took out all he could (£250 cash limit on the day. It was a Friday and he had just been paid – this is disability allowance and amounting to a two-week payout for him). Of course, they took the cash and sped off.

"What do you mean soliciting?"

"Unfortunately, by your own account, you technically solicited the young woman on the internet and then cash exchanged hands. It is your word against hers and I am giving you an opportunity, because of your vulnerability, to drop the theft case, otherwise I will have to take you in for questioning."

"So they are going to get away with it? We have CCTV at the flat and I am sure my carers will be able to find the images and I can give a really good description of the people."

"Ned, drop it. I'll pay you back. You really do not want to go to the police station to be questioned in a small room with a closed door."

"OK, Mum."

"Thank you, officer."

"As I said, my camera is off."

"That is very kind."

"I am sorry I cannot do anything else to help. There is such a racket going, internet scams, and they are so professional."

"Is that why the other officer is still in the car, because you are giving me a break?"

"Yes, young sir. Be more careful next time. Try meeting a real girl."

"Mum, Beau has built a prison – is there any more Lego?"

"Oh, how lovely. What's that bit with all the white pieces?"

"The hospital."

"And they must be the doctors."

"Uh huh."

"Ned, you have to be careful communicating with these girls online, if they are indeed girls."

"Mum?"

"Yes, Ned."

"Do you know who wrote the first short-form text-like abbreviation?"

"I think we're about to find out," says Dill.

"It was in a letter from Lord Fisher to Winston Churchill. It was OMG."

"When?"

"In 1917."

"Wow, that's early."

"To the Lighthouse," says Dill – it's our local gastro pub with a fireplace.

"Shoes on, everyone."

"Virginia Woolf, she took her own life."

"So did many great women writers, Ned, like Sylvia Plath – she was married to Laureate Ted Hughes."

"I've read *Wodwo*."

"Then there was poet Stevie Smith, she was depressed."

"Shall I give it a go?"

"No, just stick to the Bret Easton Ellis for the moment. Far less disturbing."

"OK, Mum."

"Where's Beau?"

"He's putting on a tie and wants to bring the prison with him."

"Great!"

End